MARCHES

MARCHES

for manuals

Kevin
Mayhew

We hope you enjoy the music in this book.
Further copies of this and our many other books are available
from your local music shop or Christian bookshop.

In case of difficulty, please contact the publisher direct by writing to:

The Sales Department
KEVIN MAYHEW LTD
Rattlesden
Bury St Edmunds
Suffolk IP30 0SZ

Phone 01449 737978
Fax 01449 737834

Please ask for our complete catalogue of outstanding Church Music.

Front cover illustration by Graham Johnstone
after a 1920's *Vogue* Magazine cover.

Cover designed by Jaquetta Sergeant.

First published in Great Britain in 1997 by Kevin Mayhew Ltd.

© Copyright 1997 Kevin Mayhew Ltd.

ISBN 0 86209 989 7
ISMN M 57004 051 3
Catalogue No: 1400127

0 1 2 3 4 5 6 7 8 9

Music Editor: Rosalind Welch
Music setting by Chris Hinkins

Printed and bound in Great Britain

Contents

RADETSKY MARCH

Johann Strauss (1804–1849) arr. Colin Hand

MARCH from 'THE NUTCRACKER'

Peter Ilyich Tchaikovsky (1840–1893) arr. Norman Warren

GRAND MARCH from 'AIDA'

Giuseppe Verdi (1813–1901) arr. Colin Mawby

WEDDING MARCH from SYMPHONY No 3

Camille Saint-Saëns (1835–1921) arr. Martin Setchell

MARCHE MILITAIRE

Franz Schubert (1797–1828) arr. Norman Warren